WHOLE FOODS FOR WEIGHT LC
RECIPES FOR EVERYONE

**First edition. March 19, 2024.**

ISBN: 979-8224640737

Written by Frost Melissa-Jane.

# Table of Contents

# Whole Foods For Weight Loss: Easy And Healthy Recipes For Everyone

# Lentil soup with spinach salad

## Ingredients:

- 1 cup dry lentils
- 1 onion, chopped
- 2 carrots, diced
- 2 cloves garlic, minced
- 4 cups vegetable broth
- 5 oz fresh spinach
- Salt and pepper to taste

## Equipment:

1. Pot
2. Ladle
3. Knife
4. Cutting board
5. Mixing bowl
6. Salad spinner

## Methods:

Step 1: Rinse 1 cup of lentils under cold water and set aside.

Step 2: In a large pot, sauté diced onions, carrots, and celery in olive oil until softened.

Step 3: Add minced garlic, cumin, and turmeric to the pot and cook for one minute.

Step 4: Pour in 4 cups of vegetable broth and add the rinsed lentils. Bring to a boil, then reduce heat and simmer for 20-25 minutes.

Step 5: Stir in chopped spinach and season with salt and pepper to taste.

Step 6: In a separate bowl, toss mixed greens, cherry tomatoes, and a balsamic vinaigrette for the salad.

Step 7: Serve the lentil soup alongside the spinach salad and enjoy!

## Helpful Tips:

1. Rinse lentils thoroughly before cooking to remove any dirt or debris.
2. Soak lentils for at least 2 hours before cooking to reduce cooking time.

3. Use vegetable broth instead of water for added flavor.

4. Add carrots, celery, and onions for extra depth of flavor.

5. Season soup with cumin, garlic, and lemon juice for a Mediterranean twist.

6. Serve soup with a fresh spinach salad dressed with balsamic vinaigrette.

7. Top salad with roasted nuts or seeds for added crunch.

8. Don't forget to season both the soup and salad with salt and pepper to taste.

# Baked sweet potato with grilled chicken

## Ingredients:

- 4 sweet potatoes
- 1 lb chicken breast
- Olive oil
- Salt
- Pepper
- Garlic powder
- Paprika
- Fresh herbs
- 1 lemon

## Equipment:

1. Baking sheet
2. Mixing bowl
3. Whisk
4. Grill pan
5. Tongs

## Methods:

Step 1: Preheat the oven to 400°F.

Step 2: Wash and scrub the sweet potatoes.

Step 3: Pierce the sweet potatoes with a fork and place them on a baking sheet.

Step 4: Bake the sweet potatoes in the oven for about 45-60 minutes, or until they are tender.

Step 5: While the sweet potatoes are baking, season the chicken breast with your favorite spices.

Step 6: Grill the chicken breast on a hot grill or stovetop until fully cooked.

Step 7: Once the sweet potatoes are done, split them open and top with the grilled chicken.

Step 8: Serve hot and enjoy your baked sweet potato with grilled chicken!

## Helpful Tips:

1. Preheat your oven to 400°F.

2. Wash and scrub your sweet potatoes thoroughly before baking.

3. Use a fork to pierce holes in the sweet potatoes to allow steam to escape while baking.

4. Rub the sweet potatoes with olive oil and sprinkle with salt before baking for added flavor.

5. Place the sweet potatoes directly on the oven rack and bake for 45-60 minutes, or until tender.

6. While the sweet potatoes are baking, grill your chicken with your favorite seasoning.

7. Serve the grilled chicken alongside the baked sweet potatoes for a delicious and nutritious meal.

# Egg white omelette with spinach and mushrooms

## Ingredients:
- 8 egg whites
- 2 cups spinach
- 1 cup sliced mushrooms
- Salt and pepper to taste

## Equipment:
1. Skillet
2. Spatula
3. Whisk
4. Knife
5. Cutting board

## Methods:
Step 1: Heat a non-stick skillet over medium heat.

Step 2: In a bowl, whisk together egg whites until frothy.

Step 3: Add spinach and mushrooms to the skillet and cook until tender.

Step 4: Pour the egg whites into the skillet over the vegetables.

Step 5: Allow the omelette to cook for 2-3 minutes until the edges start to set.

Step 6: Carefully fold the omelette in half using a spatula.

Step 7: Cook for another minute until the omelette is fully cooked through.

Step 8: Remove from heat and serve hot with your favorite toppings. Enjoy!

## Helpful Tips:
1. Start by whisking the egg whites until they are frothy and slightly thickened.

2. Season the egg whites with salt and pepper before pouring them into a heated non-stick skillet.

3. Cook the egg whites slowly over low heat to ensure a fluffy omelette.

4. Add chopped spinach and mushrooms on top of the egg whites before folding the omelette in half.

5. Cook the omelette for a few more minutes until the spinach and mushrooms are heated through.

6. Serve with a side of fresh fruit or whole grain toast for a complete and balanced meal.

# Roasted vegetable salad with grilled chicken

## Ingredients:
- 2 bell peppers, diced
- 1 zucchini, sliced
- 1 red onion, sliced
- 1 cup cherry tomatoes
- 1 lb grilled chicken breast
- 4 cups mixed greens
- 1/4 cup olive oil
- 2 tbsp balsamic vinegar
- Salt and pepper to taste

## Equipment:
1. Mixing bowl
2. Baking sheet
3. Grill pan
4. Tongs
5. Knife
6. Cutting board

## Methods:

Step 1: Preheat the oven to 400°F.

Step 2: Chop your favorite vegetables such as bell peppers, zucchini, and onions.

Step 3: Toss the vegetables with olive oil, salt, and pepper on a baking sheet.

Step 4: Roast the vegetables in the oven for 25-30 minutes or until they are tender.

Step 5: While the vegetables are roasting, season the chicken breast with herbs and spices of your choice.

Step 6: Grill the chicken on a hot grill until fully cooked.

Step 7: Let the chicken rest before slicing it.

Step 8: Assemble the salad with the roasted vegetables and sliced chicken on top.

Step 9: Drizzle with your favorite dressing and enjoy!

# Helpful Tips:

1. Preheat your oven to 400°F to roast your vegetables evenly.

2. Cut your vegetables into bite-sized pieces for quick and even roasting.

3. Season your vegetables with olive oil, salt, pepper, and any desired herbs or spices before roasting.

4. Use a grill pan or outdoor grill to cook your chicken breast for added flavor and texture.

5. Marinate your chicken in a mixture of olive oil, lemon juice, garlic, and herbs for at least 30 minutes before grilling.

6. Let your roasted vegetables cool slightly before tossing with fresh greens and dressing to prevent wilting.

7. Top your salad with sliced grilled chicken breast for a protein-packed meal.

# Turkey meatballs with zucchini noodles

## Ingredients:

- 1 lb ground turkey
- 1/2 cup breadcrumbs
- 1 egg
- 1 zucchini
- 1 tsp olive oil
- 1/2 tsp salt
- 1/4 tsp pepper
- 1/4 tsp garlic powder

## Equipment:

1. Frying pan
2. Mixing bowl
3. Grater
4. Knife
5. Cutting board

## Methods:

Step 1: Preheat the oven to 400°F and line a baking sheet with parchment paper.

Step 2: In a large mixing bowl, combine ground turkey, breadcrumbs, egg, garlic, onion, salt, pepper, and Italian seasoning.

Step 3: Mix the ingredients together until well combined, then form the mixture into golf ball-sized meatballs.

Step 4: Place the meatballs on the prepared baking sheet and bake for 20-25 minutes, or until cooked through.

Step 5: While the meatballs are baking, spiralize the zucchini into noodles.

Step 6: Heat a skillet over medium heat and add the zucchini noodles, cooking for 2-3 minutes.

Step 7: Serve the zucchini noodles topped with the turkey meatballs and your favorite marinara sauce. Enjoy!

## Helpful Tips:

1. Start by mixing ground turkey with breadcrumbs, minced garlic, chopped parsley, and Parmesan cheese for flavorful meatballs.

2. Use a cookie scoop to portion out even-sized meatballs to ensure they cook consistently.

3. Brown the meatballs in a hot skillet before transferring to the oven to finish cooking.

4. For the zucchini noodles, spiralize the zucchini and sauté in a little olive oil until just tender.

5. Season the zucchini noodles with salt and pepper and a squeeze of lemon juice for added flavor.

6. Serve the turkey meatballs over the zucchini noodles and top with marinara sauce and extra Parmesan cheese for a delicious meal.

# Grilled shrimp with avocado salad

## Ingredients:
- 1 lb shrimp
- 2 avocados
- 1 red onion
- 1 lime
- 1 tbsp olive oil
- 1/4 tsp salt
- 1/4 tsp pepper
- 1/4 tsp paprika

## Equipment:
1. Grill pan
2. Mixing bowl
3. Tongs
4. Whisk
5. Salad spinner

## Methods:
Step 1: Preheat the grill to medium-high heat.

Step 2: In a small bowl, mix together olive oil, lemon juice, minced garlic, salt, and pepper.

Step 3: Peel and devein the shrimp, then toss them in the olive oil mixture.

Step 4: Thread the shrimp onto skewers.

Step 5: Grill the shrimp for 2-3 minutes per side, until they are pink and opaque.

Step 6: In a large bowl, mix together diced avocado, cherry tomatoes, red onion, and cilantro.

Step 7: Add the grilled shrimp to the salad and gently toss to combine.

Step 8: Serve the grilled shrimp with avocado salad immediately and enjoy!

## Helpful Tips:
1. Start by marinating the shrimp in a mixture of olive oil, garlic, lemon juice, salt, and pepper for at least 30 minutes.

2. Preheat your grill to medium-high heat and lightly oil the grates to prevent sticking.

3. Grill the shrimp for 2-3 minutes per side, or until they are pink and opaque.

4. While the shrimp are grilling, prepare the avocado salad by combining diced avocado, tomatoes, red onion, cilantro, and lime juice in a bowl.

5. Season the salad with salt and pepper to taste, and gently toss to combine.

6. Serve the grilled shrimp on top of the avocado salad for a delicious and healthy meal.

# Tofu stir-fry with broccoli

## Ingredients:

- 1 block of tofu (400g)
- 2 cups of broccoli florets
- 2 tablespoons of soy sauce
- 1 tablespoon of hoisin sauce
- 1 teaspoon of garlic, minced
- 1 teaspoon of ginger, grated
- 2 tablespoons of vegetable oil

## Equipment:

1. Wok
2. Wooden spoon
3. Chef's knife
4. Cutting board
5. Cooking oil
6. Plate

## Methods:

Step 1: Drain and press tofu to remove excess water.

Step 2: Cut tofu into cubes and marinate with soy sauce and garlic.

Step 3: Heat oil in a pan and add marinated tofu cubes.

Step 4: Cook tofu until golden brown on all sides.

Step 5: Remove tofu from pan and set aside.

Step 6: In the same pan, add chopped broccoli and stir-fry until tender.

Step 7: Add back tofu cubes to the pan.

Step 8: Season with salt, pepper, and any other desired spices.

Step 9: Stir well to combine and cook for a few more minutes.

Step 10: Serve hot and enjoy your tofu stir-fry with broccoli!

## Helpful Tips:

1. Use extra firm tofu to prevent it from becoming mushy while stirring.

2. Press the tofu before cooking to remove excess water and improve its texture.

3. Cut the tofu into small cubes for quicker cooking and better absorption of flavors.

4. Preheat your pan or wok before adding the tofu to ensure a crispy exterior.

5. Cook the tofu on high heat to achieve a golden brown crust.

6. Add the broccoli towards the end of cooking to retain its vibrant green color and crunch.

7. Season the stir-fry with soy sauce, garlic, ginger, and red pepper flakes for a flavorful dish.

# Cauliflower crust pizza with turkey pepperoni

## Ingredients:

- 1 head cauliflower, grated
- 1 cup mozzarella cheese, shredded
- 1/2 cup parmesan cheese, grated
- 1 tsp dried oregano
- 1 tsp garlic powder
- 2 eggs
- 1/2 cup pizza sauce
- 1/2 cup turkey pepperoni slices

## Equipment:

1. Mixing bowl
2. Rolling pin
3. Baking sheet
4. Pizza cutter
5. Oven mitts

## Methods:

Step 1: Preheat the oven to 425°F.

Step 2: Cut cauliflower into florets and pulse in a food processor until it resembles rice.

Step 3: Microwave cauliflower rice for 5 minutes, then squeeze out excess water using a clean kitchen towel.

Step 4: Mix cauliflower rice with egg, shredded mozzarella, and seasonings.

Step 5: Press mixture onto a baking sheet lined with parchment paper to form a crust.

Step 6: Bake crust for 20 minutes until golden brown.

Step 7: Top with pizza sauce, shredded cheese, and turkey pepperoni.

Step 8: Bake for an additional 10 minutes until cheese is melted and bubbly.

Step 9: Enjoy your cauliflower crust pizza with turkey pepperoni!

## Helpful Tips:

1. Start by preheating your oven to the recommended temperature for baking the cauliflower crust.

2. Use a food processor to finely chop the cauliflower into rice-sized pieces.

3. Microwave the cauliflower for a few minutes to soften it before squeezing out excess moisture using a clean kitchen towel.

4. Mix the cauliflower with egg, cheese, and any desired seasonings to create the crust mixture.

5. Spread the mixture evenly on a baking sheet lined with parchment paper to form the crust.

6. Bake the crust until it is golden brown and firm to the touch.

7. Top with tomato sauce, cheese, and turkey pepperoni before baking until the cheese is bubbly and golden.

Enjoy your delicious cauliflower crust pizza with turkey pepperoni!

# Baked cod with quinoa and roasted carrots

## Ingredients:
- 4 pieces of cod fillets
- 1 cup of quinoa
- 2 large carrots
- Olive oil, salt, pepper
- Lemon wedges for serving

## Equipment:
1. Baking dish
2. Saucepan
3. Chef's knife
4. Mixing bowl
5. Sheet pan
6. Wooden spoon

## Methods:
Step 1: Preheat the oven to 400°F and line a baking sheet with parchment paper.

Step 2: Season the cod fillets with salt, pepper, and a squeeze of lemon juice.

Step 3: Place the seasoned cod fillets on the prepared baking sheet.

Step 4: In a separate bowl, mix cooked quinoa with diced roasted carrots and a drizzle of olive oil.

Step 5: Spoon the quinoa and carrot mixture around the cod fillets on the baking sheet.

Step 6: Bake in the preheated oven for 15-20 minutes, or until the cod is cooked through and flakes easily with a fork.

Step 7: Serve hot and enjoy!

## Helpful Tips:
1. Start by preheating your oven to 400°F (200°C).
2. Season the cod fillets with salt, pepper, and your favorite herbs or spices.
3. Cook the quinoa according to package instructions for a fluffy texture.

4. Toss the carrots with olive oil, salt, pepper, and any desired herbs before roasting them in the oven for about 20-25 minutes.

5. Place the seasoned cod fillets on a lined baking sheet and bake for 15-20 minutes, or until the fish is opaque and flakes easily with a fork.

6. Serve the baked cod over the quinoa with the roasted carrots on the side for a delicious and nutritious meal.

7. Garnish with fresh herbs or a squeeze of lemon juice before serving.

8. Enjoy your flavorful and healthy dish!

# Spaghetti squash with turkey bolognese

## Ingredients:

- 1 spaghetti squash
- 1 lb ground turkey
- 1 can crushed tomatoes
- 1 onion
- 2 cloves garlic
- Salt, pepper, olive oil

## Equipment:

1. Knife
2. Cutting board
3. Saute pan
4. Wooden spoon
5. Serving spoon
6. Tongs

## Methods:

Step 1: Preheat your oven to 400°F.

Step 2: Cut the spaghetti squash in half lengthwise and scoop out the seeds.

Step 3: Place the squash halves face down on a baking sheet and roast in the oven for 45-50 minutes.

Step 4: While the squash is roasting, heat a skillet over medium heat and cook ground turkey until browned.

Step 5: Add chopped onions, garlic, and diced tomatoes to the skillet and cook for another 5 minutes.

Step 6: Stir in tomato paste, Italian seasoning, salt, and pepper.

Step 7: Once the spaghetti squash is done, use a fork to scrape out the strands.

Step 8: Serve the turkey bolognese over the spaghetti squash and enjoy!

## Helpful Tips:

1. Start by preheating your oven to 400°F.

2. Cut the spaghetti squash in half lengthwise and scoop out the seeds. Place each half cut-side down on a baking sheet lined with parchment paper.

3. Roast the squash for about 40-50 minutes, or until the flesh is tender and easily pierced with a fork.

4. While the squash is cooking, prepare the turkey bolognese by cooking ground turkey in a skillet with diced onions, garlic, and crushed tomatoes.

5. Season the bolognese with salt, pepper, and Italian herbs like oregano and basil.

6. Once the squash is done, use a fork to scrape out the strands of "spaghetti" into a bowl.

7. Serve the squash topped with the turkey bolognese and enjoy!

# Grilled chicken skewers with tangy cucumber salad

## Ingredients:

- 1 lb chicken breast, cut into chunks
- 1 cucumber, sliced
- 1/4 cup Greek yogurt
- 1 tbsp lemon juice
- 1 tsp olive oil
- 1 tsp honey
- Salt and pepper to taste

## Equipment:

1. Grill pan
2. Skewers
3. Tongs
4. Mixing bowl
5. Cutting board
6. Knife

## Methods:

Step 1: Soak wooden skewers in water for at least 30 minutes.

Step 2: Cut chicken breasts into bite-sized pieces and marinate in a mixture of olive oil, lemon juice, garlic, and herbs.

Step 3: Thread chicken onto the skewers and grill over medium-high heat for 8-10 minutes, turning occasionally.

Step 4: In a bowl, combine sliced cucumbers, red onion, cherry tomatoes, feta cheese, and a tangy dressing of lemon juice, olive oil, and honey.

Step 5: Serve the grilled chicken skewers with the tangy cucumber salad on the side for a delicious and healthy meal. Enjoy!

## Helpful Tips:

1. Marinate the chicken in a mixture of olive oil, lemon juice, garlic, and your favorite seasonings for at least 30 minutes.

2. Soak the wooden skewers in water for 30 minutes to prevent them from burning.

3. Alternate threading the marinated chicken pieces onto the skewers.

4. Preheat the grill to medium-high heat before adding the skewers.

5. Grill the skewers for 12-15 minutes, turning occasionally, until chicken is cooked through.

6. Prepare the tangy cucumber salad by mixing sliced cucumbers, red onion, red wine vinegar, honey, and salt.

7. Serve the grilled chicken skewers with the cucumber salad on the side for a delicious and refreshing meal.

# Lentil curry with cauliflower rice

## Ingredients:

- 2 cups red lentils
- 1 large cauliflower
- 1 onion, diced
- 2 cloves garlic, minced
- 1 tbsp curry powder
- 1 can coconut milk
- 4 cups vegetable broth
- Salt and pepper to taste

## Equipment:

1. Knife
2. Cutting board
3. Pot
4. Skillet
5. Spatula

## Methods:

Step 1: Rinse 1 cup of lentils and soak in water for at least 30 minutes.

Step 2: In a pot, heat 1 tablespoon of oil and sauté 1 diced onion until translucent.

Step 3: Add 3 cloves of minced garlic, 1 tablespoon of grated ginger, 1 diced carrot, and 1 diced bell pepper. Cook until vegetables are softened.

Step 4: Stir in 2 tablespoons of curry powder and cook for 1 minute.

Step 5: Drain the lentils and add them to the pot with 2 cups of vegetable broth. Cover and simmer for 20 minutes.

Step 6: In a separate pan, rice cauliflower and cook until tender.

Step 7: Serve lentil curry over cauliflower rice and enjoy!

## Helpful Tips:

1. Start by sautéing diced onions, garlic, and ginger in a large pot with some oil.

2. Add in your choice of lentils (such as green, brown, or red lentils) and cover with water or vegetable broth.

3. Season with turmeric, cumin, coriander, and chili powder for extra flavor.

4. Let the curry simmer on low heat for at least 30 minutes to allow the flavors to develop.

5. In the meantime, pulse cauliflower florets in a food processor to make cauliflower rice.

6. Lightly sauté the cauliflower rice in a separate pan until tender.

7. Serve the lentil curry over the cauliflower rice for a healthy and satisfying meal. Enjoy!

# Baked chicken with quinoa and roasted vegetables

## Ingredients:
- 4 chicken breasts
- 1 cup quinoa
- 2 bell peppers
- 1 red onion
- 1 zucchini
- 2 tbsp olive oil
- Salt and pepper to taste

## Equipment:
1. Baking sheet
2. Cutting board
3. Knife
4. Saucepan
5. Roasting pan

## Methods:
Step 1: Preheat the oven to 400°F (200°C).

Step 2: Season boneless, skinless chicken breasts with salt, pepper, and your favorite herbs.

Step 3: Place the chicken on a baking sheet and bake for 25-30 minutes, or until cooked through.

Step 4: While the chicken is cooking, cook quinoa according to package instructions.

Step 5: Toss chopped vegetables (such as zucchini, bell peppers, and cherry tomatoes) with olive oil, salt, and pepper.

Step 6: Spread the vegetables on a separate baking sheet and roast for 20-25 minutes.

Step 7: Serve the baked chicken with quinoa and roasted vegetables for a healthy and delicious meal.

## Helpful Tips:

1. Marinate the chicken for at least 30 minutes to infuse it with flavor.

2. Cook the quinoa according to package instructions for the best texture.

3. Use a variety of colorful vegetables for more nutrients and flavor.

4. Preheat the oven before roasting the vegetables to ensure even cooking.

5. Season the vegetables with herbs and spices for extra taste.

6. Place the chicken on a rack while baking to allow for air circulation and crispier skin.

7. Check the internal temperature of the chicken to ensure it's fully cooked.

8. Serve with a squeeze of fresh lemon juice for a burst of brightness.

# Egg white scramble with bell peppers and onions

## Ingredients:
- 8 egg whites
- 1 red bell pepper
- 1 green bell pepper
- 1 onion

## Equipment:
1. Whisk
2. Skillet
3. Spatula
4. Cutting Board
5. Knife

## Methods:
Step 1: Heat a non-stick pan over medium heat.

Step 2: Dice one bell pepper and half an onion.

Step 3: Add the diced bell pepper and onion to the pan and sauté until they are soft.

Step 4: Separate 4 egg whites from the yolks and pour them into the pan.

Step 5: Season with salt and pepper to taste.

Step 6: Stir the eggs continuously until they are cooked through.

Step 7: Remove the pan from the heat and serve the egg white scramble with bell peppers and onions hot.

Step 8: Enjoy your healthy and delicious breakfast!

## Helpful Tips:
1. Start by heating a non-stick pan over medium heat.

2. Add chopped bell peppers and onions to the pan and cook until they start to soften.

3. In a separate bowl, whisk together egg whites with a splash of milk or water.

4. Pour the egg white mixture over the cooked veggies in the pan.

5. Use a spatula to gently scramble the eggs, cooking until they are just set.

6. Season with salt, pepper, and any other desired herbs or spices.

7. Serve hot and enjoy a healthy and delicious breakfast or lunch option.

8. Feel free to add in any other vegetables or toppings of your choice.

# Black bean soup with mixed greens salad

## Ingredients:

- 2 cans black beans
- 1 onion, diced
- 2 garlic cloves, minced
- 4 cups vegetable broth
- 1 tsp cumin
- 1/2 tsp paprika
- Mixed greens
- Cherry tomatoes
- Balsamic vinaigrette

## Equipment:

1. Chef's knife
2. Cutting board
3. Ladle
4. Mixing bowl
5. Saute pan

## Methods:

Step 1: Heat olive oil in a large pot and sauté diced onions, carrots, and celery until softened.

Step 2: Add minced garlic, cumin, and chili powder, and cook for another minute.

Step 3: Pour in vegetable broth, canned black beans, and diced tomatoes. Bring to a boil.

Step 4: Reduce heat and let simmer for 20 minutes.

Step 5: Using an immersion blender, puree the soup until smooth.

Step 6: Season with salt and pepper to taste.

Step 7: In a separate bowl, toss mixed greens with lemon juice, olive oil, and salt.

Step 8: Serve the soup with a side of mixed greens salad. Enjoy!

## Helpful Tips:

1. Start by soaking 1 cup of black beans overnight or use canned black beans for a quicker version.

2. Sauté chopped onions, garlic, and bell peppers in a pot until soft.

3. Add in the black beans, vegetable broth, cumin, paprika, and a bay leaf for flavor.

4. Simmer the soup for at least 30 minutes until the beans are tender.

5. For the mixed greens salad, toss together fresh greens, cherry tomatoes, cucumbers, and your favorite dressing.

6. Serve the black bean soup topped with a dollop of Greek yogurt or sour cream and a side of the mixed greens salad for a well-balanced meal.

7. Enjoy!

# Baked tofu with green beans

## Ingredients:

- 1 block of tofu, 1 pound fresh green beans, 2 tbsp soy sauce, 2 tsp garlic powder, 2 tsp sesame oil

## Equipment:

1. Baking sheet
2. Knife
3. Cutting board
4. Mixing bowl
5. Skillet

## Methods:

Step 1: Preheat the oven to 400°F and line a baking sheet with parchment paper.

Step 2: Press the tofu to remove excess water, then cut into cubes.

Step 3: In a bowl, mix together soy sauce, sesame oil, garlic powder, and ginger.

Step 4: Toss the tofu in the marinade until evenly coated.

Step 5: Place the tofu on the prepared baking sheet and bake for 25-30 minutes, flipping halfway through.

Step 6: Meanwhile, trim and blanch the green beans in boiling water for 2-3 minutes.

Step 7: Remove the tofu from the oven and serve with the green beans. Enjoy your baked tofu with green beans!

## Helpful Tips:

1. Press tofu before marinating to remove excess moisture and allow for better absorption of flavors.

2. Cut tofu into small cubes or slices for even cooking.

3. Marinate tofu in a mixture of soy sauce, garlic, ginger, and sesame oil for at least 30 minutes.

4. Preheat oven to 400°F and line a baking sheet with parchment paper.

5. Toss green beans with olive oil, salt, and pepper before adding tofu on the baking sheet.

6. Bake for 25-30 minutes, flipping tofu halfway through, until tofu is crispy and green beans are tender.

7. Serve with a side of rice or quinoa for a complete meal.

# Grilled tilapia tacos with lettuce wraps

## Ingredients:
- 4 tilapia fillets
- 1 head of lettuce
- 1/2 cup diced tomatoes
- 1/4 cup chopped cilantro
- 1 lime
- 1/2 tsp cumin
- 1/2 tsp garlic powder
- Salt and pepper

## Equipment:
1. Cutting board
2. Knife
3. Skillet
4. Tongs
5. Spatula

## Methods:
Step 1: Marinate tilapia fillets in a mixture of lime juice, olive oil, garlic, and spices for 30 minutes.

Step 2: Preheat grill to medium-high heat and grill the tilapia fillets for 4-5 minutes on each side.

Step 3: Warm small corn tortillas on the grill for 30 seconds on each side.

Step 4: Assemble the tacos by placing a grilled tilapia fillet on each tortilla.

Step 5: Add shredded lettuce, diced tomatoes, sliced avocado, and a dollop of sour cream to each taco.

Step 6: Serve immediately and enjoy the delicious grilled tilapia tacos with lettuce wraps!

## Helpful Tips:
1. Start by marinating the tilapia in a mixture of lime juice, garlic, and chili powder for at least 30 minutes.

2. Preheat the grill to medium-high heat and lightly oil the grates to prevent sticking.

3. Grill the marinated tilapia for about 3-4 minutes per side, or until cooked through and flaky.

4. While the tilapia is cooking, prepare your lettuce wraps by washing and drying large lettuce leaves.

5. Fill the lettuce wraps with the grilled tilapia, avocado slices, salsa, and a squeeze of fresh lime juice.

6. Serve with additional toppings like diced tomatoes, shredded cheese, and hot sauce for added flavor. Enjoy your delicious grilled tilapia tacos!

# Turkey and vegetable kebabs with quinoa

## Ingredients:

- 1 lb turkey breast, cubed
- 1 red bell pepper, chopped
- 1 zucchini, sliced
- 1 onion, chopped
- 1 cup quinoa, cooked
- 2 tbsp olive oil
- 2 cloves garlic, minced
- Salt and pepper to taste

## Equipment:

1. Skewers
2. Tongs
3. Mixing bowl
4. Grill pan
5. Knife
6. Cutting board

## Methods:

Step 1: Prepare the marinade by mixing olive oil, lemon juice, garlic, and herbs in a bowl.

Step 2: Cut turkey breast into bite-sized pieces and coat with the marinade. Let it sit for at least 30 minutes.

Step 3: Preheat grill to medium-high heat.

Step 4: In a pot, cook quinoa according to package instructions.

Step 5: Thread marinated turkey, bell peppers, onions, and cherry tomatoes onto skewers.

Step 6: Grill kebabs for 10-12 minutes, turning occasionally until turkey is cooked through.

Step 7: Serve kebabs over a bed of cooked quinoa. Enjoy!

## Helpful Tips:

1. Soak wooden skewers in water for at least 30 minutes before using them to prevent burning.

2. Marinate the turkey in a mixture of olive oil, lemon juice, garlic, and herbs for at least 30 minutes before skewering.

3. Alternate threading turkey chunks with your favorite vegetables like bell peppers, zucchini, and cherry tomatoes onto the skewers.

4. Cook the kebabs on a preheated grill or broiler for about 10-12 minutes, turning occasionally, until the turkey is cooked through.

5. Serve the kebabs over a bed of cooked quinoa for a nutritious and delicious meal. Enjoy!

# Lentil and vegetable stew with a side of broccoli

## Ingredients:

- 1 cup of dried lentils
- 2 carrots, diced
- 1 onion, chopped
- 2 cloves of garlic, minced
- 4 cups of vegetable broth
- 1 tsp cumin
- 1 tsp paprika
- 4 cups of broccoli florets

## Equipment:

1. Cutting board
2. Knife
3. Pot
4. Wooden spoon
5. Ladle

## Methods:

Step 1: Heat olive oil in a large pot over medium heat.

Step 2: Add chopped onions, carrots, and celery. Cook until softened, about 5 minutes.

Step 3: Stir in crushed garlic, cumin, and paprika. Cook for 1 minute.

Step 4: Add lentils, diced tomatoes, vegetable broth, and bay leaves. Bring to a boil.

Step 5: Reduce heat to simmer and cook for 20 minutes, or until lentils are tender.

Step 6: Meanwhile, steam broccoli until tender.

Step 7: Season the stew with salt and pepper to taste.

Step 8: Serve the lentil and vegetable stew with a side of steamed broccoli. Enjoy!

## Helpful Tips:

1. Start by sautéing chopped onions and garlic in olive oil for added flavor.

2. Add in diced carrots, celery, and bell peppers for a colorful and nutritious base.

3. Season with salt, pepper, and dried herbs like thyme and oregano for a well-rounded taste.

4. Rinse and drain the lentils before adding them to the pot with vegetable broth.

5. Let the stew simmer for at least 30 minutes to allow the flavors to meld together.

6. Steam the broccoli separately until fork-tender for a simple and healthy side dish.

7. Serve the lentil stew hot with a side of broccoli for a satisfying and nutritious meal.

# Baked sweet potato with turkey chili

## Ingredients:

- 4 small sweet potatoes
- 1 pound ground turkey
- 1 can diced tomatoes
- 1 can black beans
- 1 onion, chopped
- 2 cloves garlic
- 1 tablespoon chili powder
- Salt and pepper to taste

## Equipment:

1. Baking sheet
2. Oven
3. Potato peeler
4. Knife
5. Pot
6. Spoon

## Methods:

Step 1: Preheat your oven to 400°F.

Step 2: Wash and poke holes in a sweet potato using a fork.

Step 3: Place the sweet potato on a baking sheet and bake in the oven for 45-60 minutes, or until tender.

Step 4: While the sweet potato is baking, prepare your turkey chili by sautéing ground turkey, onions, garlic, bell peppers, and chili powder in a skillet.

Step 5: Add diced tomatoes, kidney beans, and chicken broth to the skillet and simmer for 15-20 minutes.

Step 6: Once the sweet potato is done, cut it open and top with the turkey chili.

Step 7: Enjoy your delicious baked sweet potato with turkey chili!

## Helpful Tips:

1. Preheat your oven to 400°F.

2. Scrub sweet potatoes and prick with a fork before baking.

3. Bake sweet potatoes directly on the oven rack for about 45-60 minutes.

4. While sweet potatoes are baking, prepare your turkey chili on the stovetop.

5. Make sure the turkey is fully cooked before adding in tomatoes, beans, and spices.

6. Let the chili simmer on low heat for at least 20 minutes to allow flavors to meld.

7. Once sweet potatoes are cooked through, remove from oven and split open.

8. Fill each sweet potato with a generous amount of turkey chili.

9. Top with shredded cheese, avocado, or Greek yogurt as desired.

10. Enjoy your hearty and nutritious meal!

# Egg white frittata with spinach and tomatoes

## Ingredients:

- 8 egg whites
- 1 cup chopped spinach
- 1 cup diced tomatoes
- Salt and pepper to taste

## Equipment:

1. Mixing bowl
2. Whisk
3. Skillet
4. Spatula
5. Cutting board
6. Knife

## Methods:

Step 1: Preheat the oven to 350°F and lightly grease a 9-inch pie dish.

Step 2: In a medium bowl, whisk together 8 egg whites and 4 whole eggs until well combined.

Step 3: Stir in 1 cup of chopped spinach and 1 cup of halved cherry tomatoes.

Step 4: Pour the mixture into the prepared pie dish.

Step 5: Bake in the preheated oven for 25-30 minutes, or until the frittata is set and lightly golden on top.

Step 6: Allow the frittata to cool slightly before slicing and serving. Enjoy your delicious egg white frittata with spinach and tomatoes!

## Helpful Tips:

1. Start by preheating the oven to 350°F.
2. Whisk together egg whites, a splash of milk, salt, and pepper in a bowl.
3. Heat a non-stick skillet on medium heat and add spinach and tomatoes.
4. Pour the egg white mixture over the spinach and tomatoes in the skillet.
5. Cook on the stovetop for a few minutes until the edges start to set.

6. Transfer the skillet to the oven and bake for about 10-15 minutes until the frittata is set and slightly golden on top.

7. Let it cool for a few minutes before slicing and serving. Enjoy your healthy and delicious egg white frittata!

# Grilled shrimp and vegetable skewers with cauliflower rice

## Ingredients:

- 1 lb large shrimp
- 2 zucchinis, diced
- 1 bell pepper, diced
- 1 small head cauliflower
- Olive oil
- Salt and pepper
- 2 cloves minced garlic

## Equipment:

1. Grill
2. Skewers
3. Knife
4. Cutting board
5. Bowl
6. Rice cooker

## Methods:

Step 1: Soak wooden skewers in water for 30 minutes to prevent burning.

Step 2: Preheat grill to medium-high heat.

Step 3: Thread shrimp, bell peppers, zucchini, and cherry tomatoes onto skewers.

Step 4: Drizzle skewers with olive oil, salt, and pepper.

Step 5: Grill skewers for 3-4 minutes per side, until shrimp is pink and vegetables are tender.

Step 6: In a food processor, pulse cauliflower florets until they resemble rice.

Step 7: Heat olive oil in a skillet and add cauliflower rice, cooking for 5-7 minutes until tender.

Step 8: Serve grilled shrimp and vegetable skewers over cauliflower rice. Enjoy!

## Helpful Tips:

1. Soak wooden skewers in water for at least 30 minutes to prevent them from burning.

2. Marinate shrimp in a mixture of olive oil, garlic, lemon juice, salt, and pepper for at least 30 minutes before grilling.

3. Cut vegetables into bite-sized pieces for even cooking on the skewers.

4. Don't overcrowd the skewers, leave space between each ingredient to ensure they cook properly.

5. Cook the cauliflower rice in a pan with a little bit of oil and your favorite seasonings until tender.

6. Serve with fresh herbs, lemon wedges, and a side of tzatziki sauce for added flavor.

# Tofu and vegetable stir-fry with sesame seeds

## Ingredients:
- 1 block tofu (14 oz)
- 2 tbsp sesame oil
- 2 cups mixed vegetables
- 2 tbsp soy sauce
- 1 tbsp sesame seeds

## Equipment:
1. Wok
2. Spatula
3. Knife
4. Cutting board
5. Mixing bowl

## Methods:
Step 1: Press tofu to remove excess moisture, then cut into cubes.

Step 2: Heat oil in a large skillet or wok over medium-high heat.

Step 3: Add tofu cubes and cook until golden brown on all sides.

Step 4: Remove tofu from skillet and set aside.

Step 5: Add vegetables (such as bell peppers, broccoli, and snow peas) to the skillet and cook until tender-crisp.

Step 6: Return tofu to the skillet and stir to combine.

Step 7: In a small bowl, mix together soy sauce, garlic, ginger, and sesame oil.

Step 8: Pour sauce over tofu and vegetables, stirring to coat.

Step 9: Serve stir-fry over rice, garnished with sesame seeds.

## Helpful Tips:
1. Make sure to press the tofu before cooking to remove excess moisture and allow it to absorb flavors better.

2. Cut the tofu into small cubes to ensure even cooking and maximum flavor infusion.

3. Use a high heat oil like sesame oil to stir-fry the tofu and vegetables for a nutty flavor.

4. Add vegetables that cook at similar rates to ensure everything is done at the same time.

5. Don't overcrowd the pan - cook the tofu and vegetables in batches if necessary to allow for proper browning.

6. Season with soy sauce, rice vinegar, and a pinch of sugar for a savory-sweet sauce.

7. Top with sesame seeds for added crunch and flavor before serving.

# Cauliflower crust pizza with grilled chicken and peppers

## Ingredients:

- 1 head cauliflower
- 2 eggs
- 1 cup shredded cheese
- 1 grilled chicken breast
- 1 bell pepper
- 1/2 tsp salt
- 1/4 tsp pepper

## Equipment:

1. Knife
2. Cutting board
3. Skillet
4. Mixing bowl
5. Spatula
6. Oven tray

## Methods:

Step 1: Preheat your oven to 425°F.

Step 2: Cut a head of cauliflower into florets and pulse in a food processor until it resembles rice.

Step 3: Microwave the cauliflower rice for 5 minutes, then let it cool.

Step 4: Squeeze out excess moisture from the cauliflower using a cloth or paper towel.

Step 5: Mix the cauliflower rice with 1 cup of grated cheese, 1 egg, and seasonings.

Step 6: Press the mixture onto a baking sheet lined with parchment paper to form a crust.

Step 7: Bake the crust for 15 minutes until golden brown.

Step 8: Top with grilled chicken, peppers, and more cheese, then bake for an additional 10 minutes. Enjoy your cauliflower crust pizza!

# Helpful Tips:

1. Preheat your oven to 400°F before starting the cooking process.

2. Prepare the cauliflower crust by grating a head of cauliflower and mixing it with egg, shredded mozzarella cheese, and seasonings.

3. Bake the cauliflower crust on a parchment-lined baking sheet for 20-25 minutes until it is golden brown and crispy.

4. While the crust is baking, grill seasoned chicken and sliced peppers on a grill pan until they are cooked through.

5. Once the crust is ready, top it with marinara sauce, grilled chicken, peppers, and additional cheese.

6. Bake the pizza for an additional 10-15 minutes until the cheese is melted and bubbly.

7. Let the pizza cool for a few minutes before slicing and serving. Enjoy your healthy and delicious cauliflower crust pizza!

# Baked salmon with quinoa and roasted Brussels sprouts

## Ingredients:
- 4 salmon fillets (6 oz each)
- 1 cup quinoa
- 2 cups Brussels sprouts
- Olive oil, salt, pepper
- Lemon slices

## Equipment:
1. Baking sheet
2. Mixing bowl
3. Whisk
4. Saute pan
5. Tongs

## Methods:
Step 1: Preheat the oven to 400°F.

Step 2: Rinse quinoa under cold water. In a saucepan, combine quinoa with 2 cups of water and bring to a boil. Reduce heat, cover, and simmer for 15-20 minutes.

Step 3: Toss Brussels sprouts with olive oil, salt, and pepper. Spread on a baking sheet and roast for 20-25 minutes.

Step 4: Season salmon with salt, pepper, and lemon juice. Place on a baking sheet lined with parchment paper.

Step 5: Bake salmon in the oven for 12-15 minutes.

Step 6: Serve baked salmon with cooked quinoa and roasted Brussels sprouts. Enjoy!

## Helpful Tips:
1. Preheat oven to 400°F and line a baking sheet with parchment paper.

2. Season salmon with salt, pepper, and olive oil before placing it on the baking sheet.

3. Rinse quinoa under cold water before cooking to remove any bitterness.

4. Cook quinoa according to package instructions, using chicken or vegetable broth for added flavor.

5. Toss Brussels sprouts with olive oil, salt, and pepper before roasting in the oven until browned and crispy.

6. Check salmon for doneness after 15-20 minutes or until it flakes easily with a fork.

7. Serve salmon on a bed of quinoa with roasted Brussels sprouts on the side for a balanced meal.

# Spaghetti squash with turkey meatballs

## Ingredients:

- 1 spaghetti squash
- 1 lb ground turkey
- 1/2 cup bread crumbs
- 1/4 cup grated Parmesan cheese
- 1 egg
- 1 clove garlic
- 1 tsp dried oregano
- 1/2 tsp salt
- 1/4 tsp black pepper
- 1 jar marinara sauce

## Equipment:

1. Saucepan
2. Skillet
3. Mixing bowl
4. Baking sheet
5. Wooden spoon

## Methods:

Step 1: Preheat oven to 400°F.

Step 2: Cut spaghetti squash in half lengthwise and scoop out the seeds.

Step 3: Drizzle squash with olive oil and season with salt and pepper.

Step 4: Place squash cut side down on a baking sheet and roast for 40-45 minutes.

Step 5: While squash is roasting, mix ground turkey with breadcrumbs, Parmesan cheese, egg, garlic, and Italian seasoning to form meatballs.

Step 6: Form meatballs and place on a baking sheet.

Step 7: Bake meatballs for 20-25 minutes or until cooked through.

Step 8: Use a fork to scrape out spaghetti squash strands and top with turkey meatballs and marinara sauce.

Step 9: Enjoy your spaghetti squash with turkey meatballs!

# Helpful Tips:

1. Begin by preheating your oven to 400°F.

2. Cut the spaghetti squash in half lengthwise and remove the seeds with a spoon.

3. Place the squash halves face down on a baking sheet and bake for 30-40 minutes until tender.

4. While the squash is baking, mix together ground turkey, breadcrumbs, egg, minced garlic, and seasonings to form meatballs.

5. Brown the meatballs in a skillet over medium heat.

6. Add marinara sauce to the skillet and simmer for 10-15 minutes.

7. Scrape the cooked spaghetti squash strands out with a fork and top with the turkey meatballs and sauce.

8. Enjoy your delicious and healthy meal!

# Grilled chicken Caesar salad with light dressing

## Ingredients:
- 2 chicken breasts
- 4 cups romaine lettuce
- 1/2 cup grated Parmesan
- 1/2 cup croutons
- 1/4 cup Caesar dressing

## Equipment:
1. Grilling pan
2. Salad bowl
3. Tongs
4. Whisk
5. Mixing spoon

## Methods:
Step 1: Season chicken breasts with salt, pepper, and olive oil.

Step 2: Grill the chicken on medium heat for about 6-8 minutes per side until fully cooked.

Step 3: In a large bowl, mix together romaine lettuce, cherry tomatoes, and croutons.

Step 4: For the dressing, combine light mayonnaise, lemon juice, Parmesan cheese, and Worcestershire sauce.

Step 5: Slice the grilled chicken and add it to the salad.

Step 6: Drizzle the light dressing over the salad and toss to coat evenly.

Step 7: Serve the grilled chicken Caesar salad with additional Parmesan cheese on top. Enjoy!

## Helpful Tips:
1. Marinate the chicken in a mixture of olive oil, garlic, lemon juice, and herbs for at least 30 minutes before grilling.

2. Season the chicken with salt and pepper before grilling to enhance the flavor.

3. Grill the chicken over medium-high heat for about 6-8 minutes per side, or until fully cooked.

4. Use romaine lettuce, cherry tomatoes, croutons, and shaved Parmesan cheese for the salad.

5. Make a light Caesar dressing by whisking together Greek yogurt, lemon juice, Dijon mustard, anchovy paste, and garlic.

6. Toss the salad ingredients with the dressing right before serving to keep them crisp and fresh.

# Lentil and vegetable curry with a side of cauliflower rice

## Ingredients:

- 1 cup red lentils
- 1 onion, chopped
- 2 cloves of garlic, minced
- 1 can of coconut milk
- 2 cups of mixed vegetables
- 1 head of cauliflower
- 1 tsp curry powder
- 1/2 tsp turmeric
- Salt and pepper to taste

## Equipment:

1. Saucepan
2. Skillet
3. Cutting board
4. Knife
5. Wooden spoon
6. Grater

## Methods:

Step 1: Rinse 1 cup of lentils and set aside.

Step 2: In a large pot, heat 1 tablespoon of oil over medium heat.

Step 3: Add 1 chopped onion, 2 minced garlic cloves, and 1 tablespoon of curry powder. Cook until onion is softened.

Step 4: Stir in 2 chopped carrots, 1 chopped bell pepper, and the lentils.

Step 5: Add 2 cups of vegetable broth and bring to a boil.

Step 6: Reduce heat and simmer for 20 minutes.

Step 7: In a food processor, pulse 1 head of cauliflower until rice-like.

Step 8: In a separate pan, cook cauliflower rice until tender.

Step 9: Serve lentil curry over cauliflower rice. Enjoy!

## Helpful Tips:

1. Start by sautéing onions, garlic, and ginger in a large pot with olive oil until fragrant.

2. Add in your favorite curry spices like cumin, turmeric, and coriander, then stir in diced vegetables like carrots, bell peppers, and zucchini.

3. Pour in cooked lentils and vegetable broth, simmer for about 20 minutes until vegetables are tender.

4. Meanwhile, pulse cauliflower florets in a food processor until they resemble rice grains.

5. Sauté the cauliflower rice in a separate pan with a bit of oil until tender.

6. Serve the curry over the cauliflower rice for a healthy and filling meal. Enjoy!

# Baked cod with mixed greens salad

## Ingredients:
- 4 cod fillets
- 2 tbsp olive oil
- 1 lemon, juiced
- 1 garlic clove, minced
- Salt and pepper to taste
- 4 cups mixed greens

## Equipment:
1. Baking sheet
2. Tongs
3. Mixing bowl
4. Whisk
5. Oven mitts

## Methods:
Step 1: Preheat the oven to 400°F and lightly grease a baking dish.

Step 2: Season the cod fillets with salt, pepper, and any desired herbs or spices.

Step 3: Place the cod fillets in the baking dish and drizzle with olive oil.

Step 4: Bake the cod in the preheated oven for 15-20 minutes, or until the fish is cooked through and flakes easily with a fork.

Step 5: While the cod is baking, prepare the mixed greens salad by combining your choice of mixed greens, cherry tomatoes, diced cucumbers, and a light vinaigrette dressing.

Step 6: Serve the baked cod with the mixed greens salad and enjoy!

## Helpful Tips:
1. Preheat your oven to 400°F.
2. Season your cod with salt, pepper, and lemon juice.
3. Place the cod on a baking sheet lined with parchment paper.
4. Bake the cod for 15-20 minutes, or until it flakes easily with a fork.

5. While the cod is baking, prepare your mixed greens salad with your choice of veggies, nuts, and dressing.

6. Make sure to wash and dry your greens thoroughly before assembling your salad.

7. Serve the baked cod hot with the mixed greens salad on the side for a balanced and delicious meal.

# Grilled chicken with avocado and tomato salad

## Ingredients:
- 4 boneless, skinless chicken breasts
- 2 avocados, sliced
- 2 tomatoes, chopped
- Olive oil
- Salt and pepper
- Fresh lemon juice

## Equipment:
1. Grill
2. Skillet
3. Tongs
4. Spatula
5. Mixing bowl
6. Knife

## Methods:
Step 1: Marinate the chicken breasts in a mixture of olive oil, garlic, lemon juice, salt, and pepper for at least 30 minutes.

Step 2: Preheat the grill to medium-high heat.

Step 3: Grill the chicken breasts for 6-7 minutes per side, or until cooked through.

Step 4: In a large bowl, combine diced avocado, cherry tomatoes, red onion, cilantro, lime juice, salt, and pepper for the salad.

Step 5: Toss the salad ingredients together until well combined.

Step 6: Serve the grilled chicken on a plate with the avocado and tomato salad on the side. Enjoy!

## Helpful Tips:
1. Marinate the chicken in a mixture of olive oil, lemon juice, garlic, and your favorite herbs for at least 30 minutes before grilling.

2. Make sure to preheat your grill to medium-high heat before adding the chicken.

3. Grill the chicken for about 6-8 minutes per side, or until it reaches an internal temperature of 165°F.

4. Let the chicken rest for a few minutes before slicing to allow the juices to redistribute.

5. For the avocado and tomato salad, mix ripe avocado, cherry tomatoes, red onion, cilantro, lime juice, and salt in a bowl.

6. Serve the grilled chicken with the avocado and tomato salad on the side for a delicious and healthy meal.

# Tofu stir-fry with bell peppers and snap peas

## Ingredients:

- 1 block tofu (14 oz)
- 2 bell peppers
- 1 cup snap peas
- 1/4 cup soy sauce
- 1 tbsp sesame oil
- 1 tsp ginger
- 1 tsp garlic
- 1 tsp cornstarch

## Equipment:

1. Wok
2. Stirring spoon
3. Knife
4. Cutting board
5. Strainer
6. Plate

## Methods:

Step 1: In a wok, heat oil over medium-high heat.

Step 2: Add cubed tofu and stir-fry until lightly browned.

Step 3: Remove tofu and set aside.

Step 4: In the same wok, add sliced bell peppers and snap peas.

Step 5: Stir-fry until vegetables are tender-crisp.

Step 6: Return tofu to the wok.

Step 7: Add soy sauce, garlic, ginger, and sesame oil.

Step 8: Continue stir-frying until everything is well combined and heated through.

Step 9: Serve the tofu stir-fry with bell peppers and snap peas over steamed rice or noodles.

Step 10: Enjoy your delicious and healthy meal!

## Helpful Tips:

1. Press the tofu before cooking to remove excess moisture and allow it to absorb flavors better.

2. Use firm or extra firm tofu for stir-frying to prevent it from falling apart.

3. Cut the tofu into bite-sized cubes to ensure even cooking and mixing with other ingredients.

4. Preheat the wok or skillet before adding any ingredients to ensure a good sear on the tofu.

5. Cook the tofu first until it's golden brown before adding the bell peppers and snap peas.

6. Use high heat and stir frequently to prevent sticking and ensure even cooking.

7. Season with soy sauce, ginger, garlic, and a touch of sesame oil for a flavorful dish.

# Cauliflower rice sushi rolls with avocado

## Ingredients:
- 1 small head of cauliflower
- 1 avocado
- 4 nori sheets
- Soy sauce
- Rice vinegar
- Sesame seeds
- Sriracha mayo

## Equipment:
1. Chef's knife
2. Cutting board
3. Rolling mat
4. Rice cooker
5. Bamboo steamer
6. Mixing bowl

## Methods:
Step 1: Cook 1 cup of cauliflower rice according to package instructions and let it cool.

Step 2: Lay a sheet of nori on a bamboo sushi mat and press a thin layer of cauliflower rice on top.

Step 3: Add sliced avocado, cucumber, and any other desired fillings to the center of the cauliflower rice.

Step 4: Roll the sushi tightly using the bamboo mat, moistening the edge of the nori with water to seal.

Step 5: Slice the roll into bite-sized pieces and serve with soy sauce and pickled ginger.

Step 6: Enjoy your delicious cauliflower rice sushi rolls with avocado!

## Helpful Tips:
1. Start by preparing the cauliflower rice by grating or pulsing cauliflower in a food processor until it resembles the texture of rice.

2. Season the cauliflower rice with salt and a splash of rice vinegar for added flavor.

3. Lay out a sheet of nori on a bamboo sushi rolling mat, shiny side down.

4. Spread a thin layer of cauliflower rice evenly over the nori sheet, leaving a little space at the edges.

5. Add sliced avocado and any other desired fillings, such as cucumber or carrots.

6. Roll the sushi tightly using the bamboo mat, applying pressure to ensure a compact roll.

7. Slice the roll into bite-sized pieces and enjoy with soy sauce and wasabi.

# Baked chicken with quinoa and steamed broccoli

## Ingredients:

- 4 chicken breasts
- 1 cup quinoa
- 2 cups broccoli
- Salt, pepper, olive oil

## Equipment:

1. Baking dish
2. Saucepan
3. Steamer basket
4. Mixing bowl
5. Tongs

## Methods:

Step 1: Preheat the oven to 400°F.

Step 2: Season the chicken breasts with salt, pepper, and your favorite herbs.

Step 3: Place the seasoned chicken breasts in a baking dish and cook in the oven for 25-30 minutes or until fully cooked.

Step 4: While the chicken is cooking, cook the quinoa according to the package instructions.

Step 5: Steam the broccoli until tender, about 5-7 minutes.

Step 6: Once everything is cooked, serve the baked chicken on a bed of quinoa with a side of steamed broccoli.

Step 7: Enjoy your delicious and healthy meal!

## Helpful Tips:

1. Preheat your oven to 400°F before starting to cook.

2. Season the chicken with your favorite herbs and spices for additional flavor.

3. Cook the quinoa according to package instructions for best results.

4. Steam the broccoli for 5-7 minutes, until it is tender but still slightly crisp.

5. Use a meat thermometer to ensure the chicken reaches an internal temperature of 165°F before serving.

6. Consider adding a drizzle of olive oil or a squeeze of lemon juice over the dish for extra flavor.

7. Allow the dish to rest for a few minutes before serving to let the flavors meld together.

# Veggie and egg white scramble with a side of fruit

## Ingredients:

- 8 egg whites
- 1 red bell pepper, diced
- 1/2 red onion, chopped
- 1 cup spinach
- 1 cup mixed berries

## Equipment:

1. Skillet
2. Spatula
3. Mixing bowl
4. Whisk
5. Cutting board
6. Knife

## Methods:

Step 1: Heat a non-stick skillet over medium heat.

Step 2: Add 1 teaspoon of olive oil to the skillet.

Step 3: Dice vegetables of choice (bell peppers, onions, tomatoes) and add to the skillet.

Step 4: Cook the vegetables until they are tender.

Step 5: In a separate bowl, whisk together 3 egg whites.

Step 6: Pour the egg whites into the skillet with the cooked vegetables.

Step 7: Stir the egg whites and vegetables until the eggs are cooked through.

Step 8: Serve the veggie and egg white scramble with a side of fresh fruit.

Step 9: Enjoy your healthy and delicious meal!

## Helpful Tips:

1. Start by sautéing your favorite veggies (such as bell peppers, onions, and mushrooms) in a non-stick pan with a little olive oil.

2. Once the veggies are cooked, add in your egg whites and scramble them together with the veggies until cooked through.

3. Season with salt, pepper, and any other desired seasonings (such as garlic powder or herbs).

4. Serve with a side of fresh fruit, such as a sliced orange or berries, to add a refreshing and sweet balance to the savory scramble.

5. Consider adding in some feta or goat cheese crumbles for an extra burst of flavor.

6. Enjoy your nutritious and delicious veggie and egg white scramble with fruit!

# Turkey and black bean lettuce wraps with salsa

## Ingredients:
- 1 lb ground turkey
- 1 can black beans, drained
- 1 head lettuce
- 1 cup salsa

## Equipment:
1. Knife
2. Cutting board
3. Frying pan
4. Mixing bowl
5. Tongs

## Methods:

Step 1: Heat a skillet over medium heat and add ground turkey, cooking until browned.

Step 2: Stir in black beans, corn, and salsa, allowing flavors to combine for a few minutes.

Step 3: Wash and dry lettuce leaves, then spoon turkey mixture onto each leaf.

Step 4: Roll lettuce leaves to form wraps, securing with toothpicks if needed.

Step 5: Serve with additional salsa on the side for dipping.

Step 6: Enjoy your delicious and healthy Turkey and black bean lettuce wraps with salsa!

## Helpful Tips:

1. Begin by marinating the turkey in a mixture of lime juice, cumin, garlic, and chili powder for added flavor.

2. Cook the turkey in a skillet over medium heat until fully cooked and slightly browned.

3. Rinse and drain a can of black beans before adding them to the turkey mixture for extra protein.

4. Prepare a fresh salsa by combining diced tomatoes, red onion, cilantro, lime juice, and salt.

5. Serve the turkey and black bean mixture on large lettuce leaves and top with the homemade salsa.

6. Feel free to add avocado slices or shredded cheese for additional toppings.

7. Enjoy these delicious and healthy lettuce wraps as a light and flavorful meal option.

# Lentil chili with a side of mixed greens

## Ingredients:

- 1 cup dried lentils
- 1 onion, chopped
- 1 red bell pepper, diced
- 1 can diced tomatoes
- 1 tbsp chili powder
- 1 tsp cumin
- 4 cups mixed greens

## Equipment:

1. Saucepan
2. Wooden spoon
3. Chef's knife
4. Cutting board
5. Mixing bowl

## Methods:

Step 1: Rinse 1 cup of lentils thoroughly and soak in water for 30 minutes.

Step 2: In a large pot, heat 1 tablespoon of olive oil over medium heat.

Step 3: Add 1 diced onion and 3 minced garlic cloves to the pot and sauté until onions are translucent.

Step 4: Stir in 1 tablespoon of chili powder, 1 teaspoon of cumin, and 1/2 teaspoon of paprika.

Step 5: Drain the soaked lentils and add them to the pot along with 1 can of diced tomatoes and 3 cups of vegetable broth.

Step 6: Let the chili simmer for 30 minutes, stirring occasionally.

Step 7: Serve the lentil chili with a side of mixed greens dressed with olive oil and vinegar. Enjoy!

## Helpful Tips:

1. Start by sautéing onions, garlic, and bell peppers in olive oil until softened.

2. Add in diced tomatoes, vegetable broth, and lentils, then bring to a simmer.

3. Season with chili powder, cumin, paprika, and salt to taste.

4. Let the chili cook for about 30-40 minutes, until the lentils are tender.

5. Serve the chili with a side of mixed greens tossed with a simple vinaigrette.

6. Top the chili with fresh cilantro, avocado slices, and a dollop of Greek yogurt for added flavor.

7. Enjoy a satisfying and nutritious meal perfect for meatless Fridays during Lent.

# Baked tofu with roasted Brussels sprouts

## Ingredients:
- 1 block of tofu
- 1 lb Brussels sprouts
- 3 tbsp olive oil
- Salt and pepper

## Equipment:
1. Baking sheet
2. Skillet
3. Spatula
4. Mixing bowl
5. Knife

## Methods:
Step 1: Preheat the oven to 400°F.

Step 2: Cut tofu into cubes and toss with olive oil, soy sauce, and spices.

Step 3: Spread tofu on a baking sheet and bake for 25-30 minutes, flipping halfway through.

Step 4: Trim and halve Brussels sprouts.

Step 5: Toss Brussels sprouts with olive oil, balsamic vinegar, and seasoning.

Step 6: Spread Brussels sprouts on a separate baking sheet and roast for 20-25 minutes.

Step 7: Once both tofu and Brussels sprouts are cooked, combine them in a serving dish.

Step 8: Serve hot and enjoy your baked tofu with roasted Brussels sprouts!

## Helpful Tips:
1. Preheat your oven to 400°F.

2. Press your tofu for at least 30 minutes to remove excess moisture.

3. Cut your tofu into cubes or slices for even baking.

4. Toss the tofu in a marinade of your choice, such as soy sauce, garlic, and ginger.

5. Trim and halve Brussels sprouts, then toss with olive oil, salt, and pepper.

6. Spread tofu and Brussels sprouts on a baking sheet in a single layer.

7. Bake for 25-30 minutes, flipping tofu halfway through, until tofu is golden brown and Brussels sprouts are tender.

8. Serve hot and enjoy!

# Grilled shrimp with quinoa and steamed asparagus

## Ingredients:
- 1 lb shrimp
- 1 cup quinoa
- 1 lb asparagus
- Olive oil
- Salt
- Pepper

## Equipment:
1. Grill pan
2. Pot for quinoa
3. Steamer basket
4. Tongs
5. Knife
6. Cutting board

## Methods:
Step 1: Preheat the grill to medium-high heat.

Step 2: Rinse and drain the quinoa.

Step 3: In a saucepan, bring 2 cups of water to a boil. Add the quinoa, cover, and reduce heat to low. Cook for about 15 minutes or until the quinoa is fluffy.

Step 4: Toss the shrimp with olive oil, salt, pepper, and any desired seasonings in a bowl.

Step 5: Grill the shrimp for 2-3 minutes per side or until cooked through.

Step 6: Steam the asparagus for about 5 minutes or until tender.

Step 7: Serve the grilled shrimp with the quinoa and steamed asparagus. Enjoy!

## Helpful Tips:
1. Start by marinating the shrimp in a mixture of olive oil, garlic, lemon juice, and your favorite herbs for added flavor.

2. Cook the quinoa according to package instructions, but consider using chicken or vegetable broth for added taste.

3. When grilling shrimp, season with salt and pepper and cook for 2-3 minutes on each side until pink and opaque.

4. Steam the asparagus for 3-5 minutes until tender-crisp, then season with salt, pepper, and a squeeze of lemon juice.

5. Serve the grilled shrimp on a bed of quinoa with the steamed asparagus on the side for a balanced and delicious meal.

# Turkey and vegetable stir-fry with sesame oil

## Ingredients:

- 1 lb turkey breast, sliced
- 2 tbsp sesame oil
- 2 bell peppers, sliced
- 1 onion, sliced
- 1 zucchini, sliced
- 1/4 cup soy sauce
- 1 tsp ginger, minced
- 1 tsp garlic, minced

## Equipment:

1. Wok
2. Chef's knife
3. Cutting board
4. Spatula
5. Tongs

## Methods:

Step 1: Heat a wok or large skillet over high heat.

Step 2: Add 1 tablespoon of sesame oil to the pan.

Step 3: Add 1 pound of thinly sliced turkey breast and stir-fry until cooked through.

Step 4: Remove the turkey from the pan and set aside.

Step 5: Add another tablespoon of sesame oil to the pan.

Step 6: Add 2 cups of sliced bell peppers, 1 cup of sliced mushrooms, and 1 cup of sliced carrots.

Step 7: Stir-fry the vegetables until tender-crisp.

Step 8: Return the turkey to the pan and stir everything together.

Step 9: Serve hot over cooked rice or noodles. Enjoy your delicious turkey and vegetable stir-fry with sesame oil!

## Helpful Tips:

1. Start by preparing all your ingredients beforehand: turkey breast, assorted vegetables (such as bell peppers, mushrooms, snap peas), garlic, ginger, and sesame oil.

2. Cut the turkey into thin strips and marinate it with soy sauce and a splash of sesame oil for added flavor.

3. Heat a wok or large skillet over medium-high heat and add a tablespoon of sesame oil.

4. Stir-fry the turkey until cooked through and then set it aside.

5. Add more sesame oil to the pan and stir-fry the vegetables until they are tender-crisp.

6. Add the turkey back to the pan and toss everything together with a drizzle of sesame oil.

7. Serve hot with steamed rice or noodles for a delicious and nutritious meal.

# Cauliflower crust pizza with turkey sausage and peppers

## Ingredients:

- 1 head cauliflower
- 1/2 cup shredded mozzarella
- 1/4 cup Parmesan
- 1/2 tsp salt
- 1/4 tsp pepper
- 1 egg
- 4 turkey sausage links
- 1 bell pepper
- 1/4 cup marinara sauce

## Equipment:

1. Baking sheet
2. Skillet
3. Spatula
4. Knife
5. Cutting board

## Methods:

Step 1: Preheat the oven to 425°F and line a baking sheet with parchment paper.

Step 2: In a food processor, pulse cauliflower florets until a fine texture forms.

Step 3: Microwave cauliflower for 2-3 minutes, then let it cool.

Step 4: Transfer cauliflower to a clean kitchen towel and squeeze out excess moisture.

Step 5: In a bowl, combine cauliflower, shredded cheese, eggs, and Italian seasoning.

Step 6: Press cauliflower mixture onto the prepared baking sheet to form a crust.

Step 7: Bake crust for 20 minutes, or until golden brown.

Step 8: Top with cooked turkey sausage, sliced peppers, and more cheese.

Step 9: Bake for an additional 10 minutes, or until cheese is melted. Enjoy your cauliflower crust pizza with turkey sausage and peppers!

# Helpful Tips:

1. Preheat your oven to 400°F before starting to prepare the cauliflower crust.

2. Purchase pre-made cauliflower crust to save time or make your own by using grated cauliflower, cheese, and eggs.

3. Cook the turkey sausage in a skillet until browned and crumbled.

4. Slice the peppers into thin strips and sauté them in olive oil until tender.

5. Spread marinara sauce over the cauliflower crust before adding the cooked turkey sausage and sautéed peppers.

6. Top with shredded mozzarella cheese and any additional toppings of your choice.

7. Bake in the preheated oven for 15-20 minutes or until the crust is golden brown and crispy.

8. Let cool slightly before slicing and serving. Enjoy your delicious cauliflower crust pizza with turkey sausage and peppers!

# Baked salmon with cauliflower rice and roasted carrots

## Ingredients:
- 4 salmon fillets
- 1 head cauliflower
- 4 carrots
- Olive oil, salt, pepper
- Lemon juice, parsley

## Equipment:
1. Baking sheet
2. Skillet
3. Saucepan
4. Mixing bowl
5. Wooden spoon

## Methods:
Step 1: Preheat the oven to 400°F.

Step 2: Season the salmon fillets with salt, pepper, and olive oil.

Step 3: Place the seasoned salmon on a baking sheet and bake for 12-15 minutes.

Step 4: While the salmon is baking, chop the cauliflower into florets and pulse in a food processor until it resembles rice.

Step 5: Heat a skillet over medium heat and sauté the cauliflower rice with olive oil, salt, and pepper for 5-7 minutes.

Step 6: Toss the carrots with olive oil, salt, and pepper, then roast in the oven for 20-25 minutes.

Step 7: Serve the baked salmon with cauliflower rice and roasted carrots. Enjoy!

## Helpful Tips:
1. Preheat your oven to 400°F to ensure a perfectly cooked salmon.

2. Season your salmon with salt, pepper, and your favorite herbs for added flavor.

3. Toss cauliflower rice with olive oil, garlic, and seasonings before roasting to enhance its taste.

4. Roast your carrots with a touch of honey or maple syrup for a sweet and savory twist.

5. Use a baking sheet lined with parchment paper or foil for easy cleanup.

6. Monitor cooking times closely to prevent overcooking the salmon.

7. Serve with a squeeze of fresh lemon juice for a bright citrus finish.

# Spaghetti squash with turkey and vegetable marinara

## Ingredients:

- 1 medium spaghetti squash
- 1 pound ground turkey
- 1 small onion, diced
- 1 bell pepper, diced
- 2 cups marinara sauce
- Salt and pepper to taste

## Equipment:

1. Knife
2. Cutting board
3. Skillet
4. Vegetable peeler
5. Stirring spoon
6. Baking sheet

## Methods:

Step 1: Preheat the oven to 400°F.

Step 2: Cut the spaghetti squash in half lengthwise and scoop out the seeds.

Step 3: Place the squash halves cut side down on a baking sheet and roast for 45-50 minutes or until tender.

Step 4: While the squash is cooking, cook ground turkey in a skillet over medium heat until browned.

Step 5: Add chopped vegetables (such as bell peppers, onions, and zucchini) to the skillet and cook until tender.

Step 6: Stir in marinara sauce and simmer for 5-10 minutes.

Step 7: Once the squash is done, use a fork to scrape out the strands.

Step 8: Serve the turkey and vegetable marinara over the spaghetti squash strands. Enjoy!

## Helpful Tips:

1. Start by cutting the spaghetti squash in half lengthwise and scooping out the seeds.

2. Place the squash halves cut-side down on a baking sheet and bake at 400°F for about 45 minutes, or until the flesh is easily pierced with a fork.

3. While the squash is cooking, brown ground turkey in a skillet with diced onions and garlic.

4. Add in chopped vegetables like bell peppers, zucchini, and mushrooms to the turkey mixture.

5. Stir in marinara sauce and simmer for 10-15 minutes.

6. Once the squash is done, use a fork to scrape out the spaghetti-like strands.

7. Serve the turkey and vegetable marinara over the spaghetti squash for a healthy and satisfying meal.

# Grilled chicken skewers with cucumber and tomato salad

## Ingredients:
- 1 lb chicken breast
- 1 cucumber
- 1 pint cherry tomatoes
- 2 tbsp olive oil
- Salt and pepper to taste

## Equipment:
1. Grill
2. Skewers
3. Tongs
4. Knife
5. Cutting board
6. Bowl

## Methods:
Step 1: Marinate chicken pieces in a mixture of olive oil, garlic, lemon juice, and Mediterranean spices.

Step 2: Preheat a grill or grill pan to medium-high heat.

Step 3: Thread marinated chicken onto skewers, alternating with cherry tomatoes.

Step 4: Grill skewers for 10-12 minutes, turning occasionally, until chicken is cooked through and nicely charred.

Step 5: Meanwhile, combine diced cucumber, cherry tomatoes, red onion, and feta cheese in a bowl.

Step 6: Drizzle salad with olive oil and balsamic vinegar, season with salt and pepper, and toss to coat.

Step 7: Serve grilled chicken skewers alongside cucumber and tomato salad. Enjoy!

## Helpful Tips:

1. Marinate chicken in a mixture of lemon juice, garlic, olive oil, and herbs for at least 30 minutes before grilling.

2. Soak wooden skewers in water for at least 30 minutes to prevent them from burning on the grill.

3. Alternate chicken pieces with cherry tomatoes and cucumber slices on the skewers for a colorful presentation.

4. Season the cucumber and tomato salad with salt, pepper, olive oil, and a splash of red wine vinegar for a refreshing side dish.

5. Grill the skewers over medium-high heat for 12-15 minutes, turning occasionally, until the chicken is cooked through.

6. Serve the skewers with the cucumber and tomato salad on the side for a complete and delicious meal.

# Lentil and vegetable stir-fry with a side of broccoli

## Ingredients:
- 1 cup lentils
- 2 carrots, sliced
- 1 bell pepper, diced
- 1 onion, chopped
- 2 cloves garlic, minced
- 1 head broccoli, chopped

## Equipment:
1. Skillet
2. Stirring spoon
3. Knife
4. Cutting board
5. Pot

## Methods:
Step 1: In a large skillet, heat some olive oil over medium heat.

Step 2: Add diced onions, minced garlic, and chopped bell peppers to the skillet. Cook until the vegetables are soft.

Step 3: Stir in cooked lentils, diced tomatoes, and your choice of seasonings (such as cumin, paprika, and oregano).

Step 4: Allow the mixture to simmer for 5-10 minutes, stirring occasionally.

Step 5: In a separate pot, steam or boil broccoli until tender.

Step 6: Serve the lentil and vegetable stir-fry alongside the broccoli.

Step 7: Enjoy your healthy and delicious meal!

## Helpful Tips:
1. Start by cooking the lentils according to package instructions, but make sure not to overcook them to maintain their firm texture.

2. Prepare a variety of colorful vegetables such as bell peppers, carrots, and zucchini to add flavor and nutrients to the stir-fry.

3. Use a high heat cooking oil such as avocado oil or coconut oil for stir-frying, and season the vegetables with your favorite spices or soy sauce for added flavor.

4. Cook the broccoli separately by steaming or roasting to ensure it stays crisp and vibrant.

5. Serve the lentil and vegetable stir-fry with the side of broccoli for a nutritious and satisfying meal.

# Turkey meatballs with zucchini noodles and marinara sauce

## Ingredients:
- 1 lb ground turkey
- 1/2 cup breadcrumbs
- 1/4 cup grated Parmesan
- 1 egg
- 2 zucchinis
- 1 jar marinara sauce

## Equipment:
1. Skillet
2. Mixing bowl
3. Chef's knife
4. Cutting board
5. Grater
6. Tongs

## Methods:
Step 1: Preheat the oven to 375°F.

Step 2: In a large bowl, mix together ground turkey, breadcrumbs, minced garlic, chopped parsley, salt, pepper, and egg.

Step 3: Form the mixture into golf ball-sized meatballs and place them on a baking sheet lined with parchment paper.

Step 4: Bake the meatballs in the preheated oven for 20-25 minutes, or until cooked through.

Step 5: While the meatballs are baking, spiralize the zucchini into noodles using a spiralizer.

Step 6: Heat marinara sauce in a skillet over medium heat.

Step 7: Once the meatballs are done, add them to the marinara sauce and let simmer for a few minutes.

Step 8: Serve the turkey meatballs and marinara sauce over the zucchini noodles and enjoy!

# Helpful Tips:

1. Use lean ground turkey to reduce fat content.

2. Add breadcrumbs or almond flour to turkey mixture for added texture.

3. Season turkey meatballs well with salt, pepper, and Italian seasoning.

4. Bake meatballs in the oven instead of frying for a healthier option.

5. Use a spiralizer to make zucchini noodles for a low-carb alternative to pasta.

6. Saute zucchini noodles in olive oil and garlic for added flavor.

7. Choose a low-sugar marinara sauce to keep the dish healthy.

8. Add fresh herbs like basil or parsley to garnish before serving.

9. Consider adding grated Parmesan cheese for extra flavor.

# Baked sweet potato with grilled chicken and mixed greens

## Ingredients:

- 2 large sweet potatoes
- 1 lb grilled chicken
- 6 cups mixed greens
- Olive oil, salt, and pepper

## Equipment:

1. Knife
2. Cutting board
3. Baking sheet
4. Oven
5. Grill pan
6. Salad tongs

## Methods:

Step 1: Preheat the oven to 400°F.

Step 2: Wash and scrub sweet potatoes, then pierce them with a fork several times.

Step 3: Place sweet potatoes on a baking sheet and bake for about 45-60 minutes, or until tender.

Step 4: Season chicken breasts with salt, pepper, and your favorite seasoning.

Step 5: Grill chicken on medium-high heat for about 6-8 minutes per side, or until fully cooked.

Step 6: Let chicken rest for a few minutes before slicing.

Step 7: Toss mixed greens with your favorite dressing.

Step 8: Serve baked sweet potatoes topped with sliced grilled chicken and mixed greens. Enjoy!

## Helpful Tips:

1. Preheat your oven to 400°F.

2. Scrub the sweet potatoes clean and pierce them with a fork before baking for 45-60 minutes or until tender.

3. Marinate the chicken breasts with your favorite seasoning and grill them until cooked through.

4. Toss mixed salad greens with a light vinaigrette dressing for a refreshing side dish.

5. Top your baked sweet potato with butter, salt, and pepper for added flavor.

6. Serve the grilled chicken sliced on top of the sweet potato and greens for a balanced meal.

7. Garnish with fresh herbs or a squeeze of lemon for an extra burst of flavor.

# Black bean soup with a side of arugula salad

## Ingredients:
- 2 cans black beans
- 1 onion
- 2 cloves garlic
- 1 tsp cumin
- 4 cups vegetable broth
- 4 cups arugula
- 1 lemon
- 2 tbsp olive oil

## Equipment:
1. Pot
2. Pan
3. Knife
4. Cutting board
5. Ladle
6. Mixing bowl

## Methods:
Step 1: Rinse 1 cup of black beans and soak in water overnight.

Step 2: In a large pot, sauté chopped onion, garlic, and red bell pepper until soft.

Step 3: Add the soaked black beans and cover with vegetable broth.

Step 4: Bring to a boil, then reduce heat and simmer for 1-2 hours until beans are tender.

Step 5: Blend soup until smooth, then season with cumin, chili powder, and salt to taste.

Step 6: For the arugula salad, toss arugula with lemon juice, olive oil, salt, and pepper.

Step 7: Serve soup with a side of arugula salad. Enjoy!

## Helpful Tips:
1. Start by soaking black beans overnight, or use canned beans to save time.

2. Saute onions, garlic, and bell peppers in a large pot before adding the beans and broth.

3. Add spices like cumin, paprika, and chili powder for flavor.

4. Let the soup simmer for at least 30 minutes to allow the flavors to develop.

5. While the soup is cooking, prepare a simple arugula salad with a lemon vinaigrette dressing.

6. Serve the soup hot with a dollop of sour cream or avocado slices on top.

7. Pair with the refreshing arugula salad for a balanced meal. Enjoy!

# Baked cod with quinoa and roasted green beans

## Ingredients:

- 4 cod fillets
- 1 cup quinoa
- 2 cups green beans
- Olive oil
- Salt and pepper
- Lemon juice

## Equipment:

1. Baking dish
2. Saucepan
3. Skillet
4. Baking sheet
5. Colander

## Methods:

Step 1: Preheat the oven to 400°F and line a baking sheet with parchment paper.

Step 2: Rinse the cod fillets and pat dry with paper towels.

Step 3: Season the cod with salt, pepper, and a drizzle of olive oil.

Step 4: Place the seasoned cod on the baking sheet and bake for 15-20 minutes, or until the flesh flakes easily with a fork.

Step 5: While the cod is baking, cook the quinoa according to package instructions.

Step 6: Toss the green beans with olive oil, salt, and pepper on a separate baking sheet.

Step 7: Roast the green beans in the oven for 15-20 minutes, or until tender.

Step 8: Serve the baked cod over the quinoa with a side of roasted green beans. Enjoy!

## Helpful Tips:

1. Preheat your oven to 400°F before starting to cook.

2. Season the cod fillets with salt, pepper, and your favorite herbs or spices.

3. Cook the quinoa according to package instructions for the best results.

4. Toss the green beans with olive oil, salt, and pepper before roasting.

5. Arrange the cod fillets on a baking sheet lined with parchment paper to prevent sticking.

6. Bake the cod for about 15-20 minutes or until it flakes easily with a fork.

7. Check the green beans halfway through cooking and toss to ensure they cook evenly.

8. Serve the baked cod on a bed of quinoa with the roasted green beans on the side for a balanced and delicious meal.

# Grilled tilapia tacos with lettuce wraps and salsa

## Ingredients:

- 4 tilapia fillets
- 1 head of lettuce
- 1/2 cup salsa
- 1 tbsp olive oil

## Equipment:

1. Grill
2. Tongs
3. Knife
4. Cutting board
5. Mixing bowl

## Methods:

Step 1: Preheat grill to medium-high heat.

Step 2: Season tilapia fillets with salt, pepper, and any desired spices.

Step 3: Grill tilapia fillets for 4-5 minutes on each side, or until cooked through.

Step 4: While tilapia is cooking, prepare the lettuce wraps by washing and drying lettuce leaves.

Step 5: Once tilapia is cooked, flake the fish into bite-sized pieces.

Step 6: Fill each lettuce leaf with flaked tilapia and top with salsa.

Step 7: Serve the grilled tilapia tacos with lettuce wraps and salsa. Enjoy!

## Helpful Tips:

1. Start by marinating the tilapia in a mix of lime juice, garlic, and chili powder for at least 30 minutes.

2. Preheat your grill to medium-high heat and oil the grates to prevent sticking.

3. Grill the marinated tilapia for about 4-5 minutes per side until cooked through and flaky.

4. While the fish is cooking, prepare your lettuce wraps by washing and drying the lettuce leaves.

5. Mix diced tomatoes, red onion, cilantro, jalapeno, and lime juice to make a fresh salsa topping for the tacos.

6. Fill the lettuce wraps with grilled tilapia and salsa before serving.

7. Enjoy your healthy and delicious grilled tilapia tacos!

# Turkey and vegetable kebabs with cauliflower rice

## Ingredients:

- 1 lb turkey breast, cubed
- 1 bell pepper, sliced
- 1 zucchini, sliced
- 1 onion, diced
- 1 head cauliflower, riced
- 2 tbsp olive oil
- 1 tsp cumin
- 1 tsp paprika
- Salt and pepper to taste

## Equipment:

1. Skewers
2. Cutting board
3. Knife
4. Grilling pan
5. Mixing bowl

## Methods:

Step 1: Soak wooden skewers in water for at least 30 minutes to prevent them from burning.

Step 2: Cut turkey breast into bite-sized cubes and chop vegetables of your choice into similar sizes.

Step 3: Season the turkey and vegetables with olive oil, lemon juice, garlic, and herbs of your choice.

Step 4: Thread the turkey and vegetables onto the soaked skewers, alternating between the ingredients.

Step 5: Preheat grill to medium-high heat and grill the kebabs for 10-15 minutes, turning occasionally until cooked through.

Step 6: While the kebabs are cooking, prepare cauliflower rice according to package instructions.

Step 7: Serve the turkey and vegetable kebabs with cauliflower rice and enjoy!

# Helpful Tips:

1. Marinate the turkey chunks in a mixture of olive oil, lemon juice, garlic, and herbs for extra flavor.

2. Choose a variety of colorful vegetables like bell peppers, zucchini, and red onion for a visually appealing kebab.

3. Soak wooden skewers in water for at least 30 minutes before threading on the ingredients to prevent burning.

4. Cook the cauliflower rice with a bit of olive oil, garlic, and salt for added taste.

5. Grill or bake the kebabs until the turkey is fully cooked and the vegetables are slightly charred.

6. Serve the kebabs on a bed of cauliflower rice for a low-carb and healthy meal option.

# Lentil and vegetable stew with a side of roasted cauliflower

## Ingredients:
- 1 cup lentils
- 2 carrots, chopped
- 1 onion, diced
- 2 cloves garlic, minced
- 4 cups vegetable broth
- 1 head cauliflower, chopped

## Equipment:
1. Pot
2. Pan
3. Knife
4. Cutting board
5. Wooden spoon

## Methods:
Step 1: Rinse and drain 1 cup of lentils, then set aside.

Step 2: In a large pot, heat olive oil over medium heat.

Step 3: Add diced onions, carrots, and celery to the pot, sauté until vegetables are tender.

Step 4: Stir in minced garlic, cumin, and paprika, cook for 1 minute.

Step 5: Add lentils, diced tomatoes, vegetable broth, and bay leaves to the pot.

Step 6: Bring to a boil, then reduce heat and simmer for 25-30 minutes.

Step 7: While stew is simmering, preheat oven to 400°F and toss cauliflower florets with olive oil and seasonings.

Step 8: Roast cauliflower for 20-25 minutes, until golden brown.

Step 9: Serve lentil stew with a side of roasted cauliflower. Enjoy!

## Helpful Tips:
1. Start by sautéing onions and garlic in olive oil until fragrant.

2. Add chopped carrots, celery, and bell peppers to the pot for extra flavor and nutrients.

3. Rinse and drain the lentils before adding them to the pot with vegetable broth.

4. Season with your favorite spices like cumin, paprika, and thyme for a tasty stew.

5. Let the stew simmer for at least 30 minutes to allow the flavors to develop.

6. While the stew is cooking, toss cauliflower florets with olive oil, salt, and pepper before roasting in the oven.

7. Serve the lentil and vegetable stew with the roasted cauliflower for a satisfying and nutritious meal.

# Baked sweet potato with turkey chili and a side of mixed greens

## Ingredients:

- 2 large sweet potatoes
- 1 lb ground turkey
- 1 can diced tomatoes
- 1 can black beans
- Mixed greens

## Equipment:

1. Baking sheet
2. Oven mitts
3. Pot
4. Ladle
5. Salad tongs

## Methods:

Step 1: Preheat the oven to 400°F and line a baking sheet with parchment paper.

Step 2: Wash and scrub sweet potatoes, then pierce with a fork several times.

Step 3: Place sweet potatoes on the baking sheet and bake for 45-60 minutes until tender.

Step 4: While sweet potatoes are baking, prepare turkey chili according to recipe.

Step 5: Wash and chop mixed greens for the side salad.

Step 6: Once sweet potatoes are cooked, slice them open and fill with turkey chili.

Step 7: Serve the stuffed sweet potatoes with a side of mixed greens.

Step 8: Enjoy your delicious and nutritious meal!

## Helpful Tips:

1. Preheat your oven to 400°F and wash your sweet potatoes before baking.

2. Pierce the sweet potatoes with a fork a few times before placing them on a baking sheet.

3. Cook the sweet potatoes for 45-60 minutes or until they are tender.

4. While the sweet potatoes are cooking, prepare your turkey chili on the stovetop.

5. Make sure to season the chili with your favorite spices such as chili powder, cumin, and garlic.

6. Once the sweet potatoes are done, top them with the turkey chili and any additional toppings you prefer.

7. Serve with a side of mixed greens tossed in a light vinaigrette for a balanced meal. Enjoy!

# Egg white scramble with bell peppers, onions, and spinach

## Ingredients:

- 8 egg whites
- 1 bell pepper
- 1/2 onion
- 2 cups spinach

## Equipment:

1. Skillet
2. Spatula
3. Knife
4. Cutting board
5. Mixing bowl

## Methods:

Step 1: Heat a non-stick pan over medium heat.

Step 2: Add diced bell peppers and onions to the pan and cook until they start to soften.

Step 3: Add a handful of spinach to the pan and cook until wilted.

Step 4: In a separate bowl, whisk together the egg whites until frothy.

Step 5: Pour the egg whites over the vegetables in the pan.

Step 6: Cook, stirring occasionally, until the eggs are fully cooked.

Step 7: Season with salt and pepper to taste.

Step 8: Serve hot and enjoy your delicious egg white scramble with bell peppers, onions, and spinach.

## Helpful Tips:

1. Start by heating a non-stick skillet over medium heat.

2. Whisk together 4-6 egg whites in a bowl until frothy.

3. Chop up bell peppers, onions, and spinach finely.

4. Add a small amount of olive oil to the skillet and sauté the veggies until they are softened.

5. Pour the egg whites over the veggies in the skillet.

6. Stir the mixture constantly until the eggs are cooked through.

7. Season with salt, pepper, and any other desired seasonings.

8. Serve hot and enjoy your healthy and delicious egg white scramble!

# Grilled shrimp and vegetable skewers with quinoa

## Ingredients:
- 1 lb shrimp
- 2 zucchinis
- 1 red bell pepper
- 1 red onion
- 1 cup quinoa
- Olive oil
- Salt
- Pepper

## Equipment:
1. Grill
2. Skewers
3. Tongs
4. Pot
5. Knife

## Methods:
Step 1: Soak wooden skewers in water for 30 minutes.

Step 2: Preheat grill to medium-high heat.

Step 3: In a large bowl, toss peeled and deveined shrimp with olive oil, garlic, salt, and pepper.

Step 4: Thread shrimp onto skewers, alternating with cherry tomatoes, bell peppers, and zucchini chunks.

Step 5: Grill skewers for 2-3 minutes per side, or until shrimp is cooked through and vegetables are tender.

Step 6: In a saucepan, bring quinoa and water to a boil. Reduce heat, cover, and simmer for 15 minutes.

Step 7: Serve grilled shrimp and vegetable skewers over quinoa and enjoy.

## Helpful Tips:

1. Marinate the shrimp in a mixture of olive oil, garlic, lemon juice, and your favorite seasonings for at least 30 minutes before grilling.

2. Cut vegetables like bell peppers, zucchini, and cherry tomatoes into similar-sized pieces to ensure even cooking on the skewers.

3. Precook the quinoa according to package instructions before skewering it with the shrimp and vegetables.

4. Soak wooden skewers in water for at least 30 minutes before assembling to prevent them from burning on the grill.

5. Grill skewers over medium-high heat for around 5-7 minutes per side, or until shrimp is pink and vegetables are tender.

6. Serve hot with a sprinkle of fresh herbs and a squeeze of lemon juice for added flavor. Enjoy!

# Tofu and vegetable stir-fry with teriyaki sauce

## Ingredients:
- 1 block of tofu (400g)
- 2 cups of mixed vegetables
- 4 tbsp of teriyaki sauce
- 2 tbsp of vegetable oil

## Equipment:
1. Wok
2. Wooden spatula
3. Mixing bowl
4. Cutting board
5. Knife

## Methods:
Step 1: Press tofu to remove excess moisture and cut into 1-inch cubes.

Step 2: Heat oil in a large skillet over medium-high heat.

Step 3: Add tofu cubes and cook until browned on all sides, about 5 minutes.

Step 4: Remove tofu from skillet and set aside.

Step 5: Add sliced bell peppers, broccoli florets, and sliced carrots to the skillet and cook until slightly softened, about 3-4 minutes.

Step 6: Return tofu to the skillet.

Step 7: Pour teriyaki sauce over tofu and vegetables.

Step 8: Cook for an additional 2-3 minutes, stirring occasionally.

Step 9: Serve hot over rice or noodles. Enjoy!

## Helpful Tips:
1. Use extra firm tofu for stir-frying as it holds its shape better.

2. Press the tofu before cooking to remove excess water and help it absorb flavors better.

3. Cut the tofu into bite-sized cubes for even cooking.

4. Preheat the pan before adding tofu to prevent sticking.

5. Add vegetables that cook at similar times to ensure even cooking.

6. Use a mix of colorful vegetables for a visually appealing dish.

7. Add teriyaki sauce towards the end of cooking to prevent it from burning.

8. Taste and adjust seasoning as needed before serving.

9. Serve over cooked rice or noodles for a complete meal.

# Cauliflower crust pizza with grilled chicken and tomatoes

## Ingredients:

- 1 head of cauliflower
- 2 eggs
- 1 cup shredded mozzarella cheese
- 1/2 tsp salt
- 1/4 tsp pepper
- 1 grilled chicken breast
- 1 cup cherry tomatoes

## Equipment:

1. Mixing bowl
2. Baking sheet
3. Knife
4. Cutting board
5. Saucepan

## Methods:

Step 1: Preheat the oven to 425°F.

Step 2: Cut the cauliflower into florets and pulse in a food processor until it resembles rice.

Step 3: Microwave the cauliflower rice for 5 minutes, then let cool.

Step 4: Wrap the cauliflower rice in a clean kitchen towel and squeeze out excess moisture.

Step 5: In a bowl, combine the cauliflower rice, mozzarella, Parmesan, egg, and seasonings.

Step 6: Form the cauliflower mixture into a pizza crust on a baking sheet lined with parchment paper.

Step 7: Bake the crust for 15-20 minutes, until golden brown and firm.

Step 8: Top with grilled chicken, tomatoes, and any other desired toppings.

Step 9: Bake for another 10 minutes, until toppings are heated through.

Step 10: Slice and enjoy your cauliflower crust pizza with grilled chicken and tomatoes.

# Helpful Tips:

1. Preheat your oven to 425°F.

2. Start by making the cauliflower crust by grating cauliflower and mixing it with eggs, cheese, and seasonings.

3. Spread the cauliflower mixture onto a baking sheet lined with parchment paper to form a crust.

4. Bake the crust for 15-20 minutes until it starts to brown and set aside.

5. Grill seasoned chicken breast until fully cooked, then slice it thinly.

6. Top the cauliflower crust with tomato slices, grilled chicken, and any other desired toppings.

7. Return the pizza to the oven and bake for an additional 10-15 minutes.

8. Slice and serve hot. Enjoy your healthy and delicious cauliflower crust pizza!

# Lentil and vegetable curry with cauliflower rice

## Ingredients:
- 1 cup red lentils
- 1 onion, chopped
- 2 cloves garlic, minced
- 1 can diced tomatoes
- 1 cup vegetable broth
- 1 tsp curry powder
- 1 head cauliflower, riced
- 4 cups mixed vegetables

## Equipment:
1. Knife
2. Cutting board
3. Pot
4. Wooden spoon
5. Pan
6. Mixing bowl

## Methods:
Step 1: In a large pot, heat 1 tablespoon of olive oil over medium heat.

Step 2: Add 1 diced onion and 2 minced garlic cloves, sauté until fragrant.

Step 3: Stir in 1 tablespoon of curry powder, 1 teaspoon of ground cumin, and 1 teaspoon of ground turmeric.

Step 4: Add 1 cup of diced carrots, 1 cup of diced bell peppers, and 1 cup of diced tomatoes.

Step 5: Pour in 2 cups of vegetable broth and 1 cup of red lentils.

Step 6: Bring to a boil, then reduce heat and simmer for 20 minutes.

Step 7: In a food processor, pulse cauliflower florets until rice-like consistency.

Step 8: In a separate pan, heat 1 tablespoon of olive oil and add cauliflower rice.

Step 9: Sauté for 5-7 minutes until tender.

Step 10: Serve the lentil and vegetable curry over cauliflower rice. Enjoy!

# Helpful Tips:

1. Start by sautéing diced onions and garlic in a large pot with olive oil until softened.

2. Add in diced carrots, celery, and bell peppers for added flavor and nutrients.

3. Stir in diced tomatoes, vegetable broth, and rinsed lentils. Bring to a boil, then reduce heat and simmer until lentils are tender.

4. Season with curry powder, turmeric, cumin, and salt to taste.

5. While the curry simmers, prepare the cauliflower rice by pulsing cauliflower florets in a food processor until rice-like consistency.

6. Sauté cauliflower rice in a separate pan with a drizzle of olive oil until tender.

7. Serve the lentil and vegetable curry over the cauliflower rice for a wholesome and satisfying meal. Enjoy!

# Cauliflower rice sushi rolls with avocado and cucumber

## Ingredients:

- 1 head of cauliflower
- 1 avocado
- 1 cucumber
- 4 nori seaweed sheets

## Equipment:

1. Knife
2. Cutting board
3. Rolling mat
4. Rice cooker
5. Bamboo sushi mat

## Methods:

Step 1: Start by making the cauliflower rice by pulsing cauliflower florets in a food processor until they resemble rice grains.

Step 2: Spread out the cauliflower rice on a baking sheet and bake in the oven at 375°F for 10-15 minutes.

Step 3: Lay out a sheet of nori on a bamboo sushi mat and spread a thin layer of cauliflower rice over the nori.

Step 4: Add thinly sliced avocado and cucumber on top of the cauliflower rice.

Step 5: Carefully roll up the sushi using the bamboo mat, applying gentle pressure to seal the roll.

Step 6: Cut the roll into bite-sized pieces and serve with soy sauce and pickled ginger. Enjoy your cauliflower rice sushi rolls!

## Helpful Tips:

1. Start by making your cauliflower rice by pulsing cauliflower florets in a food processor until fine.

2. Spread the cauliflower rice on a baking sheet and bake at 400°F for 15-20 minutes to remove excess moisture.

3. Let the rice cool before using it for your sushi rolls.

4. Lay a sheet of nori on a bamboo sushi mat with the shiny side facing down.

5. Spread the cauliflower rice onto the nori, leaving a 1-inch border at the top.

6. Add sliced avocado and cucumber on top of the rice.

7. Roll the sushi tightly using the bamboo mat.

8. Cut into bite-sized pieces and enjoy!

Milton Keynes UK
Ingram Content Group UK Ltd.
UKHW020738010424
440421UK00014B/872